Want, the Lake

Want, the Lake

poems

༜

JENNY FACTOR

🐓 Red Hen Press | *Pasadena, CA*

Book design by Mark E. Cull

Library of Congress Cataloging-in-Publication Data

Names: Factor, Jenny, 1969– author.
Title: Want, the lake: poems / Jenny Factor.
Other titles: Want, the lake (Compilation)
Description: First edition. | Pasadena, CA: Red Hen Press, 2024.
Identifiers: LCCN 2024006049 (print) | LCCN 2024006050 (ebook) | ISBN
    9781636281643 (paperback) | ISBN 9781636281650 (ebook)
Subjects: LCGFT: Poetry.
Classification: LCC PS3606.A26 W36 2024 (print) | LCC PS3606.A26 (ebook)
    | DDC 811/.6—dc23/eng/20240208
LC record available at https://lccn.loc.gov/2024006049
LC ebook record available at https://lccn.loc.gov/2024006050

The National Endowment for the Arts, the Los Angeles County Arts Commission, the Ahmanson
Foundation, the Dwight Stuart Youth Fund, the Max Factor Family Foundation, the Pasadena
Tournament of Roses Foundation, the Pasadena Arts & Culture Commission and the City of
Pasadena Cultural Affairs Division, the City of Los Angeles Department of Cultural Affairs, the
Audrey & Sydney Irmas Charitable Foundation, the Meta & George Rosenberg Foundation, the
Albert and Elaine Borchard Foundation, the Adams Family Foundation, Amazon Literary Part-
nership, the Sam Francis Foundation, and the Mara W. Breech Foundation partially support Red
Hen Press.

First Edition
Published by Red Hen Press
www.redhen.org

Acknowledgments

Thanks to the following journals where some of these poems first appeared:

Academy of American Poets, Alabama Literary Review, Antioch Threads, Beloit Poetry Journal, Drunken Boat, Harrington Lesbian Fiction Quarterly, Margie, *Ms. Magazine, Poetry Daily, Poetry Magazine Online, Prairie Schooner, Sinister Wisdom.*

"Sapphics on Nursing" also appeared in *The Poet's Child* (ed. Michael Wiegers, Copper Canyon Press, 2001) in a slightly different form. "For I Have Washed Your Jeans and New Embroidered Shirt" appeared in *Wide Awake: Poets of Los Angeles and Beyond* (eds. Suzanne Lummis, Liz Camfiord, Henry J. Morro, Beyond Baroque Books, 2015). A section of "Why Flood? Why Shadow? A Confession & a Covenant" appeared in *Milk and Honey: A Celebration of Jewish Lesbian Poetry* (ed. Julie R. Enszer, A Midsummer Night's Press, 2011). "Song Beside a Sippy Cup" appeared in Poetry 180 (ed. Billy Collins, Random House, 2003) and *Phoenix Rising: The Next Generation of Formal Poets* (ed. Sonny Williams, Textos Books, 2004).

Thanks to the Arroyo Arts Collective for putting "For I Have Washed Your Jeans and New Embroidered Shirt" in a laundry shop window, and to composer Melika M. Fitzhugh for honoring several of my poetic lines and stanzas with musical works: "A woman keeps opening," "splattering rose and ripple," and "Between Prognostication and Doubt."

This book has sailed a long way thanks primarily to my mother, Susan Gornel Factor, who lifted me up to beauty, who held onto all my words, and always kept a pen in her purse, and my dapper father, Max Factor III, who showed me by lesson and example that it could be a *good* thing to see the world a bit differently. I am grateful as well to my extended family and friends in life and poetry: Colleen Rooney and Eloise Klein Healy, David Lehman and Stacey Harwood Lehman, Marilyn Hacker, Melika M. Fitzhugh, Patrick Sylvain, Julie Enszer, Jennifer Jahner, and numerous students and colleagues at California Institute of Technology, Brandeis University, and Antioch University Los Angeles. Steve Heller, over twelve years, never let me forget to put poetry first. With lyric skill and smarts, Jennifer Sweeney helped me see the pattern in the cloth and Elaina Ellis held up the kindest mirror. My college friends sustained me in ways too deep to name. To my colleagues and friends at Red Hen Press: thank you for sacrificing to support the community so many writers draw strength from. Kate, Mark, Tobi: you cheered early drafts and believed in my work even when I believed I needed to change it. Daniel Gornel (z'l) told me to hurry; he loved poetry (and me) and had so wanted to live to see this book into print. Jane Factor keeps reminding me with her searching questions that poetry matters. Elena Abascal brought us all new joy. And Gail Libman (z'l) taught me to listen to my lakes harder and more generously, a lesson in laughter and self-compassion I never want to stop learning. Countless friends trekked to readings. And as always and in everything that I am, this is for my son, Lev.

for Gail Libman

Contents

Wanting   17

i left myself

apogee   21

Fruits & Vegetables   22

Sinking   23

Want the Lake   24

In August   31

The Modern Lotus Eaters   32

we eat to remember

Shiny Penny   35

Elegy for a Younger Self: Walking in the Snow   37

What I never understood about my mother's body   40

Mother: Verbed and Snared   42

I remade myself for several hours   48

Elegy for a Younger Self: Road Trip with Lakes   50

How I Want to Hold You   52

here is the story

Bear Bare Skin: a snow white rose red story

  1. The Field Speaks to the Reader   57

  2. Rose Tells the Field about Another Field . . .   58

  Interlude: Bear Enters the Home of Snow and Rose   60

  3. Bear Explains Their Clothing to Rose and Snow   61

  4. Snow Defines Love and the Purpose of Silence   63

  5. Wizard Speaks, Making Clear His Intentions   65

  6. Bear Warns Snow and Rose about the Wizard   66

  7. Rose and Snow Tell the Field Their Troubles   67

we unmake every gesture

Diagnosis   71

The Last Resort   73

On Choosing, and Not Choosing   74

Why Flood? Why Shadow? A Confession & a Covenant   76

For I have washed your jeans and new embroidered shirt . . .   82

i almost spoke i never spoke

Ode to New Leisure: Technology   85

Scenes Abroad   86

Serpent's Tooth   87

On Not Aiming for What You Really Want   88

Sapphics on Nursing   90

Diptych   92

The Song of the Sippy Cup   93

Contingency, Irony, Ingenue-ity   94

my own sound a water

Mama   97

Pep Talk   98

A Mother's Headache   100

Descent to the Pt. Reyes Lighthouse   101

Death Valley Pupfish   104

Notes from the Other Side   105

Settling In   108

twice i grew that tiny heart

Amma's Love Lesson   111

Ode to Old Leisure: Of Boredom   113

The Phone Call   114

165 Cambridge Park Drive, Day 2   115

there is no end to it

Recitativo   119

She Said to Me   120

Letter in (. . .), Threes, Fives, and Sixes 121

Pen Pals   124

Romantic Friendship   125

Spider   126

Nest (recipe)   127

Reciprocal?   128

a confession & a covenant

Passing Through   131

People Ask What I Do   135

Joanna at 2 o'clock   136

Malibu Noël   139

Against Publishing   142

Notes   143

Want, the Lake

"Then he sorrowed . . . and the sorrow did not deceive him; it did all it could for him and in the sweetness of sorrow he possessed his disappointed expectation."

—Soren Kierkegaard

Wanting

O Desire. I don't want the cup. I want
The lake.

i left myself

apogee

Effigy of darkness, darkening
Sorrow. A container of dreams.
The dreaming awaken, container
Of lustless, how the lustless imagine.
They poise on the doing, always
Not doing. Rain on a sea cleft,
Rain on a cliff face. The darkness
Of wit. The wetting of darkness.
I came and I came. I came and
You loved me. Rain in the windows;
And the clock hand descended.

Fruits & Vegetables

for Bob Bowen

Who will speak of the fruit
Abundant in the summer harvest?
This guy on the corner of San Gabriel

And First, wearing his red baseball cap
backward, salutes us with a bag
Of silent cherries and leaps into traffic

With a jaunty hand. Who will speak
Of crates of oranges ripened on the tree,
Of the great waves of zucchini

Trucking to the markets. And when the markets
Turn them away, the workers who take in
These fruity orphans and lift them up

On each summer corner
Like a flag, like a shield, like some
Dangling offer of surrender?

In median strips
Beside shut SUV windows,
Along the routes of endless going

These orphans and these vegetables,
These fruits and this harvest
In our country, in our America

Who will name this sweet abundance? this
Crop of summer
Ripening on each corner.

Will you speak? Will you?

Will I?

Sinking

After a poem and a line by J.P. Dancing Bear

In the kitchen light, she was at the sink
Dabbing at a large stack of plates with a pocked pink
Sponge, holding a fry pan, that black cake

of iron, a weight in one hand.
From the slant/catch of her shoulders, back
toward him, he could tell he'd forgotten

something   Like a promise . . . an anniversary . . . his own
name   And he looked through his pockets for it
As he laid   a kiss on the downy neck,

those fine little vulnerable hairs
He loved her, but prepared himself aware
for the slap   Of everything he'd forgotten

in her unturning back.   Hello, he tested. Her "hello"
a grunt back   Angry, but not angry enough for a scene
Good day, he tested, wondering whether "hard day"

would do more   Earn him at least a small score
that he'd considered that sad alternative to the more personal
invective, the mad shoulders, unturning hair.   She continued continuing

standing there   And soon   he was sinking in it
the stone silence. All he could not do.   And the night
a night of No things   Ancient   Cliff-faced   Blue

Want the Lake

let this darkness be a belltower / and you the bell
—Rilke, *Sonnets to Orpheus* (trans. Joanna Macy)

I. The Bell: Visiting my friends,

I hold the scuffed old sheep's bell in my hand
in a field on the coldest morning of the year

Little leather finger. Little leather fist of
knotted rope around a corded metal bell, growing

warm. Its heft. Its hollow song.
What are its neighbors, its family, this sound?

Well, the lighthouse, and the seeds of a dried
and shaken gourd, and the sound

of our sea on a black and rocky shore. It's a difficult
sound. Nobody's easy. A tethered

rustle-and-ring that speaks
on movement, snapping wandering thought

to attention, snapping the little dog to attention too
and the person standing on a midwinter morning

along the side of a stony road, or beside a frozen
edge of a building, where grates breathe warmth

up into the vacant city streets. As if snapping the flags
to attention too, and in the fields, far out, the cows and sheep.

Who would want to be the animal that makes a bell
rattle as it moves: Look at me. Look at me.

Certainly not the sheep, the soft and
rough wooly breathing angels. The sheep would rather

slip in and out of grasses they love
on their very bellies like the snake. The bell's sound and legs

bind the lamb to chilly, unwelcoming air,
the substance of what's empty, vapid, cold.

How would it feel to wear around one's neck
this small bauble, this brass babbling acorn

with the faint scent of blood. Inert, unhosted,
the brass bell is like a freedom, a slain

thing. Yet what is the guilt of this poor trinket?
Only to ride loudly and with a waving attention—

little trickster, little parade, a small child intent
on its own rattling—a host made

for the hush and clipped sound of grass
and the quietest hoof-falls from barn to meadow.

What is a bell's vibration? I've moved it
so gently in my palms that I can feel the ball

within it roll to the edge of its house
and every surface wants to whisper out to

every other like a hug. So my mother. Mother
whose lap would take me in a guilt graceful

as ground. Her nose in my hair and my tears
(yes, my tears had done it) had allowed her soft

hold to *hover hush hum me* like this for a little while . . .

II. The Bell & the Rigging

When I was a small child, they sent me to Maine
one summer to learn to be hard on myself

Eight for eight weeks. No ten, really. (But the heart
lies true.) So when I was ten (let's get the facts right)

I went to camp where the woods and lake
and the strange-and-always shedding birches

took the place of parents, household
home. The games we played in that small

pressure cooker, our bunk: an entire
government under coup. Lies lying true. And

the only place I seemed to have that thing
I knew as *self* was at the edge of the lake,

cords slapping against the masts of
the anchored boats with a rattle and a rustle

like the sheep's bell. *I want to go.* But you
must stay. *I want to go.* But you must stay.

The wind would belabor this conversation
with the line of furled sails, and I with my own self,

as the lake lapp-lapped with its hungry tongue
and the day so new, with only I in it. And

I vowed then, as I vowed every morning,
that I would never love anyone again.

But I did love again. At camp, inside the art dome
I loved a counselor, from a music school,

for the way she would look up at me as she played
her notes, and behind the dank gymnasium, watching

the tall tumblers, wanting *in*
with my eyes and hope, and all-in

and warm, on a mattress, perched
above Cambridge February, tucked in snow,

then tank-topping the spring, the fresh grass calling to me
out the classroom window. And next,

in a marriage bed, and later, on a cot
under a window all sliced through

by a wise tree, a silken necklace
around a tawny neck dangling

so low it brushed my own belly. I loved
with my lips alive and my breath, then on my knees,

then with my hands. I loved under the ache of loss
and less. Understand: whenever I loved,

no matter who I loved, I pealed out of myself,
I left myself: a brassy, shiny call.

III. The Rigging:

If want is a lake, I learned to sail in it,
in the dog days of Autumn, after the sailing

coach, Mary, got banished for going down
on a slender, dark-haired counselor

under the downturned metal bodies
of the trim canoes. We all tried to picture them

under there together, not sure how those two
bodies would go together, move. Our own

bodies unsexed still, and near
one another, suntan lotion, shaving cream,

as many genders as the weather, and wanting, wanting.
That afternoon, Hannah

flipped backside front Mary's pre-test sailing
board. Showed us finally how to free cords

from mast and raise the fishes' gasping lung
into the air. Then while my jangly boat

flipped and flopped on its strip of sand, Hannah
motioned me aside, "you know, Mary

wanted so much to tell you goodbye."
This odd fact jangled, like the sail's mast,

restlessly in my mind.

❧

Understand, a young girl starts to want for nothing
real. Wants to hear herself sound out

like a season or a song. Starts to keep
winter and summer in the same deep pocket

of weather and regret. Somehow sweet
and also wrong. Wants to get

as far away as possible from the small and powerless
shadows that scuttle and stow themselves

with no gender, standing as they do on one leg
like angels, or lying belly-flat on the wood

floor. Understand, in the depths of my being, I
was this keening: all hell, no blind and wooly home.

❧

Jennifer lay down on the trim skiff, her long
legs dangling in the froth, and I took the island

in a haul. Blueberries to the left, and all day
to pick them. Karen and Robin

in the boat to our right. Whom I could overtake,
drafting. Who rode where the summer breeze sent.

Over the sundashed firmament. Water. Island. Boat house.
Water. Waves. All forgiven in the lazy flow

we rode like a borrowed day. The four of us
climbed the hill together, back to our bunk

in the trees. There was some distant ringing in the breeze.

I want to go. *But you must stay.* I want to go.
But you must stay. And through the years, those

Messages argued inside me, while deeper in,
I just stood still, I waited patiently

                   mawing quietly   the supple, the yielding grass.

In August

The August river shrivels up and dries.
Dives into leaves and never tumbles out.
In stale, hot air, it hears the Summer lie:
This is the end, and nothing green gets out.

In spring, the river swells too deep to move,
So full of cold it overflows its sides
To eat the wet dirt with a hungry mouth
And swallow whole what Winter let survive.

Most times, the river's river: running sure
And sleek and clear, it races on and on
exhaustless, cold and clean, and free of hope,
An endless leaving all can count upon.

But this is also river: pebbles worn
To round and smooth, no gauge or fret
The leaf that, getting caught, will rot to peat
The rock that turns back water, like regret.

The Modern Lotus Eaters

for Eugenia and Brian

We eat to remember, not forget
We eat the flat hands of the pond
We eat the grass till grass is gone
The plant is bitter, fibrous, green.
We taste the night slick on our tongues.
We swallow up the fog and dirt.
Our bellies, hard with ancient chert.
With fragrant Anne's lace, snowy queen.
We eat as quickly as we can:
crisp Autumn leaves that scuffle on.
We eat the glances that are gone.
We eat the silence of a street.
Our lives point backward, swallowing sleep,
for only what we eat, we keep.

we eat to remember

Shiny Penny

for Jenifer, Madelaine, Margaret, and Sarah

Do you ever want to lose something of immense value
        irrationally,

as if losing makes you weightless

makes the sunset double   life

      in its fullness finally comfort you

How time might entirely stop then,

a loss so complete.   as if you, yourself were what's fallen
settling on a pavement,

or maybe just drifted up,
        to a pavement made of cloud

where you could stare
         up   or   through and out
until Mother Real come find you,

come pick you off
  that pavement,
say,

there you are
my Penny. My Shiny Disk of Want.

I am here.
Your Time Mother. I am
here to hold on to your "all-you've-been-forgetting"

at long last, my sparkling dear,
  You have at last slipped away from what-owns-you
    Come up off the scuffed pavement
into My circle of Joy
    you are finally, finally found!

Elegy for a Younger Self: Walking in the Snow

Walking in the snow with vodka hot in my throat (because,
    you know, there were parties)

Walking in the snow with Tom
Walking in the snow after dark   lying down   making snow
                                   angels.

Walking in the snow in wet coats, that smelled like
                    wet dogs, leaning them
        against the space heater and talking.

Walking on the path   walking and talking   as fast as we could
walking in the heat of the conversation
    in the snow   on the path
that was not as big as   the path   (because of the snow)
that was only as big as
        the-path-through-the-snow

In the heat of the conversation
knowing which one of us had to drop back a little
    so that the conversation
could continue, then jog a little
    so the conversation could continue   side-by-side

Walking in the snow   between   historic buildings

Walking in the snow and one of the buildings was Mind
Walking in the snow with one of the buildings was *mine*.

Walking by the doors made of brick
                    made of Archway made of Life
                    walking

Walking by the doors to the buildings with the stairs
the glass doors
and upstairs
the party
and the vodka hot in her throat

Dancing on the roof
                                                as the snow fell
Dancing on the roof in the snow
        Dancing on the roof   knowing it was high
        and contained fell
within it

and then down the stairs and walking

Walking and climbing and walking and talking and
climbing
and the scarves off
and the knit gloves off
each with their depth their crust of snow

and it was midnight, or near it, or dawn or near it,
        or noon noon noon bright white
with snow   and we were 18   we were 18   and everything
ahead of us was new, every single thing ahead of us
                was new

and so we climbed to the top of the belltower,
time after time,
                or maybe
                only that

         one time

and   Tom and I   we looked out

                         over Boston,

looked out

  over the sparkly,

          litup

     snowed-under

  Boston

as if

              everything we saw

every single solitary thing   we saw

could be

      ours

What I never understood about my mother's body

for my grandmothers

What I never understood about my mother's body
Was how sweet she'd smell after a bath

How the soft and cream of her gathered in the steam
Pillow mirrors everywhere

Then she'd lift herself out, a moist, fertile mountain
High and broad and in the air

And then, she was a drama made of hair
Tugging the brush through thick dyed strands

The blower a hot wind, and me, at the doorway
Wanting to touch it.   And my talking to her:

"Can I wear your dress one day."
—*No, love, we're not the same shape.*

I was a sponge of love for her.
I was wet like I'd been dipped in the soapy sink

warm and wearing my coat of bubbles
thinking in shapes and figures

as children think; language a silken skein,
impressions bouncing off streaming air

And again my mother at the table
And again, me standing behind her chair

And the hairspray setting everything in place
the hairspray acrid and precise

Sometimes I imagine there was a ladder
from my childhood to the woman I'd wanted to be

and I still walk around that old house
looking for someone to hold it steady for me

Mother: Verbed and Snared

I feel trapped, I told my first love
Three weeks into our engagement.
I had dreamt of wings taken
from my body, and laid
on a lawn chair. I could not
get them back on.

"What?" he asked, perfectly calm.
Trapped, I said,
in a little house—you and me.

"No," he'd clucked. "Marriage isn't
a tiny house, it's a large mansion,
and there are rooms in there for everything—
for the way we read in the evenings,
and for you to cook breakfast
in your bathrobe then sing at the sink,
there's a room for your anger, and one
for mine, and several rooms for being
alone. And if we're ever trapped
in that house, Jen, then I promise
we'll build a new wing."

Wing of house, wing of bird.

Reader, I married him.

I had dreamed of a life clean of compromise
a life I held in my hands
and owed nobody
a life that no one carried
for me—not even for a little while

     Instead an infant fastened
     to the dawn of my breathing
     I hungered through the crying
     nights, my body going faster & faster
     than any mind could reach   The restlessness

     was wicked then   as tensile as bitter
     as softened apples, giving way under foot, under field

My mother said, "What war is
to a man, a baby is to a woman,"
by which she meant,
I would learn

to defer the self
to watch someone else's back
to practice a sort of gallows humor

Right. And indeed, at the end of the day, the solo trip
to the mailbox felt like a safari retreat,
a spa, escape. And there was that self I carried
with me everywhere—not the baby, but just me—
its debilitating errors—
spitup-stained and dog tired.

Sometimes (I felt like a corn husk)
Other times I couldn't help but laugh.

～

But Mother too is a role, a fiction. A story well told. A shattered cocoon.

The face of the mother appears and disappears
In the hummingbird the carton of milk the fresh soup the silk slip the dear friend
—my *own* son—

Mother is a verb, a function, that keeps getting saddled with its noun.

How friable the mind; let's map every fissure:
One self for the market, another for the bath
And another wakes at six a.m. so there will be a ladle in my hand at breakfast

Watching every pancake take on form.

﹌

so *arma virumque cano*, o husband

I sing of arms like an octopus
arms that can carry a toy truck the size
of a small dog and still butter
a child's bread before drinking
her coffee. I sing of arms
that can carry a sleeping 40 lb. child
whose head is as heavy
as trust. I sing of the woman
warm in her night robe, her
warmth ancient beside you, whose
breasts make a little oven
against which she likes to hold things
like a small frozen foot or a bath-
wrinkled thumb. I sing of arms as angry
as an engine while she pushes
the steel edge of a grocery basket
that seems to wail of its own accord.

I sing of briars in her throat and
pebbles in her pocket, a candy wrapper
from a lollipop she didn't herself
eat. I sing *the carseat is heavy,* o husband.
I sing that the mule follows. Her skirts are
brown, a kind of fur. Her jacket has
snail trails that cover each shoulder.
She is a terrible soldier, carrying its
burden too plain to see.

∾

But Reader,

If the woman is a noun at 20,

at 40, she's a verb; if at 20 a bird, at 40 a net.

And so praise the dry and the wet.

Praise the far-flung thing and the mooring place.

(wings and shoes are often made of Air)

Praise the mule, the butterfly.

Praise the beautiful snare.

I remade myself for several hours

for Judith

I remade myself for several hours
in the quiet consecration of sales.
All those selves on hangers, shelves;
the low voices of shopkeepers

brushing my ears. The kiss of fabric—
satin, gauze. My body sheathed
and unsheathed like a sword.
I am potent now. The owner

of bags that dangle dazzlingly
from each hand. Behind me, a quiet
shop closes its doors. On this February twilight,
these lives rebeginning—with the

chain mail of businesses shut down,
the whispers of shopkeepers, those watchers.
I am always turning
my back on some possibility

I could have bought simply
with these two coins I saved—
Out of habit? For a lover? For
the me-I-meant-to-be

to arrive. Twilight says, "Go home.
It's beginning." The murmur
of harvest soup on the burner inside
and a child's voice asking a question

whose answer must be improvised
in smoke and memory gathered
from air. Lay the bags by the door
and Listen. (Do you *hear* it?) Where

all is habitual, the folded
question mark, Possibility,
is also here.

Elegy for a Younger Self: Road Trip with Lakes

for Stephanie Glazier, who also visited Crater Lake

That week when we hiked into crumbling hills,
he turned over each fossiliferous slate, while
I was trying to remember who I was
I was trying not to lose
my footing, stones sliding beneath us
like dinner plates.

Then in the huffing mornings beside the lake
Campfire coffee, a warmth in the cup

I knew nothing then of middle distances—
how to love without smothering, without diving head
first toward the breast, nose pushed in tight, breath leaving
breathless for that milk
In the morning, I'd wake beside him,
our red sleeping bags tangled at the root
and hold myself there,
as the muscle-memory returned to me,
how to unzip the flap, to head out, to leave.

I would lie on the edge, thinking back to sleep,
My nights were sliced with knife edges.
I was naked then, off and on.
I was naked often.
I was wholly alive, but
I was not yet even a woman beside him
And he, a boy, sucking the rock-hard candy of our hope,
his pockets filled with our powerbars

One night, a logging truck
chugged beardlike beside us
on the highway, narrow and dark
their shadows a calligraphy of logs and light
And us in our car, looking for the campground,

an inroad, Dylan on the stereo
and all those words, woods, words
struggling in my throat

Eventually, we pulled over and
turned off our headlights
And just watched that log truck moving back and forth
like a turtle, its trailer a sweeping circle
in the dark, having lost its route, re-finding it
refining it: native, destroyer.
I almost spoke. I never spoke.

Motor off, he looked up star-drunk,
and I looked and looked too
into the emptiness of galaxies, all that
light and dark and wavelength, a timeshift's falsity of perspective.
Our silence held the silence of windows.

Each morning, more and more
tendrils of my hair kept slipping out of
my French braid. I swept them back, my
slender fingers prodding, tucking
into that soft net.

How all that long week,
I bared my tan shoulders
and turned my open face
toward the lens
turned open my face
toward the lens, waiting for
something to soften me, waiting for
whatever was coming next:

One blue photo after another
One blue day after another blue dazzling day

How I Want to Hold You

for FPB

In a great clarity
Like a turbine slicing wind

Elastically, like skin holds a tattoo
Temporarily, like gravel clings to tires

Not as close as a rag doll
Not small in my hand like a stone
Not tight like a nickel
Not an object at all

In the shadows of a doorway, between prognostication and doubt
In the shifting light, like a lighthouse seeks out what's solid
In the storm's eye, how dust is pixelated against the skin

Softly, like the sun holds warmth in the sand
Kindly, like the sky holds rain to a flower

Under the freeway underpass, with my collection of broken carts
and wet socks washed up like flotsam around us

In the particle of you, with your range of wavelengths
In my own full range of sizes and places

Kaleidoscopically, and able to turn over, to
turn the image, or the idea over, to turn the dream over and over,
the shifting language of us over and over

Two planets, in their rotations, whose orbits bless one another.

Gravitationally.
As I want you. As I want to hold. As still me myself.

And not only in arms, but in my thoughts.

How do I want to hold you? How do I really already
hold you? Constantly, yet at that

perfect distance, where you can breathe, where I can let you

here is the story

Bear Bare Skin: a snow white rose red story

When you are transformed into something else,
everything becomes optional . . .
    —Danielle Stanard

Here is a story of corn and cottonwood
of Rose red and Snow white, and the wild things
of the forest, of the wild things, of the forest . . .

1. The Field Speaks to the Reader

Something hopeful is moving through the forest.
Its coat is the color of burlap maps.
There is no animal that is female the way

a human woman is female. What does this say
about the human woman? the animal? Something hopeful
is moving through the forest whose duality

makes something happen. Will you open
your door? What will you find there? A terrible happiness
is having its way with the grass. The grasses know what I mean

that no animal that is female the way a human woman
is female. This bear has size and amplitude.
—"Snow white and Rose red, don't beat your lover

Dead," a crone calls out to them. Something
hopeful is knocking at the door, sounding like
a windstorm. Here

in a gold dress and fur coat, a tough tall body
and steel-trap mind, knocking at
the storm-drift door. Like fur, like spring

entering . . .

2. Rose Tells the Field about Another Field . . .

There is a cornfield where the bodies of children are found
I have planned my trip

Because I have a child who is missing her body
All awake inside this self with breasts and eyes

In a land where all the eyes are twinkling like peepshow windows
I have planned my trip

Out to where a hand is folded over a heart, inert
like a handkerchief

Where shadows sleep like pent-up seeds, with bent-up knees,
under the satin underslip of skin

Where a boy was bound, where a girl found
a child-formed-child with polka dots of dirt

between those toes, her hightops off, his lace-top socks, yellow
where the pee hit,

and the light bottoms up, grimy and pink,
stopped in rivers, toeing the stony stream

light-up shoes, mud-crusted,
a place the objects rest—comb and doll's head,

backpack and child chair, emptied of their
empathies, their innocence and wild, untamed becomings,

Out to the cornfield of innocence and terror
Where Noelle was bound, Matthew lost, found,

where Elizabeth was, before she came back to us
Fished out of the tundra of our imaginations

Surely in that cornfield there is something for me, some damaged flesh
I can fold my soul inside

Some meat of childhood not yet turned
to crow

Interlude: Bear Enters the Home of Snow and Rose

<,;'   <,;'   <,;'   <,;'
   <,;'   <,;'   <,;'   <,;'

%%&   %%&

    %%&   I come from the forest, from that field of trouble

I come from the body   that field
                     of trouble
                          Here

3. Bear Explains Their Clothing to Rose and Snow

I love to run my fingers through my bear skin coat
I will be warm enough as I wander through the woods
All you really need is a good myth
And a snow maiden with a warm fire

I love how the maiden strokes my bear skin coat
As I rest my sleepy head by her fire
she stares into my eyes, blank with sleep
the moment before the moment of surrender

I dream of hummingbirds and bumble bees—that myth
an enclosed garden thick to my knees in British ivy
while the fire warms up my bear skin coat
and I am inside it, that question mark

I hear the night is minus 2 with an ice-glass wind
I hear I will end up sleeping in the forest
Sleeping where the roots and moss meet and cover me
The moths visit me but forget me

Something there is that does not love a bear skin coat
Its fur as soft as eiderdown
Its fur a friction of fitness and finesse
Its fugacity sleek as water's

So I wander through the forest with a bear skin coat
In a borrowed dress the color of marigold and cinnamon
Thank God I have my thick skin and my bear skin coat
Such a thin dress, all crepe paper and myrtle

Would snow love me if she found me in my bear skin coat
Would rose leave me by the corn and the ice-crust grass
Who would take this shadow from my eyes, as blank as myth
And empty these pockets of triple horn and surrender

4. Snow Defines Love and the Purpose of Silence

for my bear

Sometimes the mind wants to shudder off its coat of words
and sentences

The pre-word place in the throat, the chest—
always in a state of wonder or terror   wonder & terror
How beautiful you are where you cannot say.
How beautiful you are—complete in your surrender.

How beautiful you are where I cannot say:
Humiliation in the throat like fur, like feathers
You will know the truth when you feel it in the tube of inside
Burrowing down toward the wood chips of surrender

You will know the truth when I cannot lift my eyes
your truth heavy as a fur coat on my shoulders
the wafer of God stopping up my tongue
and your hands choking on the eloquence of surrender

I love you, Bear, and so I love
the woods and the preamble, the marigold dress
you wear, your fur and the firs, the water
in our fire. How a curse is a costume for escape, for fleeing.

Each night when I bring you my trouble.
Each night when your trouble warms our space,
I can see the light of the fire
reflected by your warmth, and in your face.

There is nothing to say to this love,
nothing to say of us, so whole.
I breathe the white dream of the dawn.
You breathe the steam-breath of the foal.

5. Wizard Speaks, Making Clear His Intentions

I am not at all small just small-minded
Have you ever felt your thoughts winnow like a sieve?
I am the magnet that pulls you out of where you live
I am a red sack, hollow-winded

To winnow: to chafe off what is chaff
To wind-up: wind in the windsock of a red sack
I am the magnet at your back
I know the place where the earth is rank and soft

Gratitude? I've never known any
I pull myself from all the mud I meet
Gold coins jangle from my ankles, I stomp them with my feet
Whether copper or fool's gold or only pennies

No matter. My name is mud. Yours? You haven't any
not where the frogs sing the names of the lost
I know exactly what a precious thing costs.
Tell me is there anything not precious to someone. Any?

I will not let go of cursing. I will never bless.
I know all the traps. I spring all that's sprung.
I am mean, steel-minded and high-strung.
You hear me. But you will never hear me confess.

Those girls . . . I've seen them. What can they do for me.
That Bear . . . I've cursed him. He's dead(named).
Who will even know? Song . . . I've stomped on it.
Believe me. Believe. Wearing me out . . . hearing me out . . .

6. Bear Warns Snow and Rose about the Wizard

Have you seen the man with the money pot
He is distracted. He is wicked.
He has left me with this thick coat of flesh
A soft vehicle of caress, a soft vehicle

Of escape. For fleeing. If you do not speak
To the mage, he will not hurt you
It's the gold he is after. He will even
Give you gifts. From his leftovers.

And so here I am, with this
Bear skin coat, and not a gold
Penny in my pocket. And we all know
Where the gold is, and where

The gold is, nothing
worth having.

7. Rose and Snow Tell the Field Their Troubles

They say we slayed the mage, but we didn't have the courage.
They say Snow married Bear, and Rose, Bear's brother.
It isn't true. That story is just hollow.
We find ourselves every evening again in this field.

Like Isaac. Like Esau. The survivor. The hunter.
Who saw too much truth with their eyes. Went blind.
We like to wander through the field, the dusk
a kind of prayer, we pray because we are half-alive, are alive

Walking among the doll parts. The old shoes. Instead . . . we are
walking by a fur coat, stripped daily of more flesh.
Snow of silence couldn't learn to bless.
I of speech could never find my solace. (Or is it silence . . . ?)

And that fur coat fell off in the ice cut grass
as the body left the body. Those who work the fields,
who harvest what the field yields, harvest up
souls and souls. The small mage is small-hearted forever.

The forest holds to the forest's curse.
There is no body of triple horn and surrender.
So throw out the carpet, don the musky sweater.
Sweep up the wood floors with a broom and pan.

Every part of a woman can be held in your hands:
even marigold. Even lavender. So . . . remember.
Marry these small parts to the bigger story:
We all wake alone at the end of December.

we unmake every gesture

Diagnosis

for E.R.R.

For a long time
after we knew,
the news
was both true
and untrue

Each day,
simple; sunrise,
its dagger edge
of red, axed
through us

then
the leafspears,
all tip and
heartbreak
It was

the keening
that
anticipated
keening.
we walked on

the path
under its bed
of fog and
feathers,
   the baby

still close against my chest
breathing his
still sweet
butter breath

the ax of what
was falling
hadn't
fallen yet.

The Last Resort

Not during the flight, but after, I remember us talking about Love,
that night as we wandered the beach, our bunny racing ahead of us
and back, ahead and back in the sand, until from above our shoulders,
a heron landed. Do you know how a night heron on a beach looks into
what seems to be a Wailing Nothing? The black body of feathers,
standing in the wind, ruffles a little, like a skirt lifts off, or the way
a baby sighs just before sleep. Not peaceful like that,
but piecemeal, inadvertent; like a shrug inside the self
away from the self. Yes, *that*. The night heron
landing like Night on the post. And in our ears, the metal chains
of the stacked beach chairs, clanging. And on that post,
Night's dark emissary landing like a dark on top of the dark that roiled
and sighed and swept and unswept, full of everything primordial,
in God's uncreated universe.
                        The heron gazed into all of it,
with his magic fisher's eye, seeing not Chaos but *sustenance, sustenance . . .*

When we reached the end of the beach, we stopped. When we
reached the end of the beach, you put a large moist hand on my shoulder.
And I don't know why but in the middle of that warmth, I felt such a deathly
rage boil up in me,   like a summer storm, hot and deep. And I don't blame
the sleeplessness, nor the month we'd spent weaning,
nor even how tenderness felt after such a long sorrow. It was just
standing there beside the clean arrow of your goodness in the face
of all that chaos, and how I knew then that whatever I wished for,
I could never save us from myself.
And I wanted so much for those two young lovers to get away, for us
to lift right out of our bodies and fly somewhere safe; somewhere
like an island at six a.m. when the clouds lift up just a little
and the day sings; where the sun could rise for us
morning after morning
around that
little house of dreams where first we imagined we could become a family.

On Choosing, and Not Choosing

On a dirt road, against a night sky, lost and looking
for the guest house, we stopped to watch

a dirigible   orange with flame   rise up
above Saugatuck   umbering down

on Lake Michigan petals of behindness.
The night was dark round a lifting planet

that could have been our whole world:
Just hurricane and lightness,

filled with a kind of longing, loping
into the translucent flush of stars—

Was I expecting my life to suddenly come out
clear? So translucent as sheets,

this line, my life. No. This was not a balloon
for standing in. Rather, a dream balloon,

set in motion. Human, to wish to set things
in motion: Like kites, this flight

lifts up, while we stay, grounded.
Most days, my senses are fogged over. A friend

asks, *Did you hear that* and I have to remind
myself—oh yes, you must have meant the traffic

like a great swan-swoosh in the distance. Or
a train whistle knifing like a harmonica

under the crickets   while time eats
the tail I trail behind, memory fumbling

the data, like two women from Choloma
by the side of a dark road, of a desert extending

into more blind night who stand needing
what will come   needing salvation

knowing the high headlights might be
more knife than hope,   and so nod,   wave them

closer,   all the while   covering their eyes,
so as not to see death coming for them

or for their children. And so isn't this better. One self
behind.   Not doing Not yet.

The senses in their now, numbed through, though
while ahead of me and extending out

that other self, translucent, possible
plump and impotent on its own waterlogged becoming.

And this is the trick and how it forgives us: to live Liminal;
in false wholeness.

Everything narrowing toward the moment for choosing:
the leaving, without the loss yet in it.

Why Flood? Why Shadow? A Confession & a Covenant

after Yehuda Amichai

I need to love you, perhaps, by contrast *not* comparison—
    You: seacliff
    Me: flood tossed
    Me: seacliff
    You: flood tossed
I need to love you, perhaps, by contrast *and* comparison—

           ॐ

I wake as always in our house—our rectangle house—our boat
    with the seaspray
          and the jangle of sails, the canvas
          awning outside our room—
          whose kitchen
          is a steaming engine, whose living room
    is hollow and strut.   In the stomach
of a huge sailing ship, whose bedroom
sways like bunks on a journey, whose dining room is another
    canvas sail, a jib, that catches
          all the winds
          of the neighborhood—the baby moaning
          and giggling, the boy sleeping,
          and the neighbors on their front lawns,
    at their front doors, exchanging   bread and vinegar and peaches,
the tricycles spinning with that plastic scraping sound   the rattle and clack of mowers.

       I wake in my life, the boat.

           ॐ

              My lover is like
              that sunbaked
              boat owner
              who tends the skiff

with skill and
soap, who devotedly
sands down
the old paint chips
who replaces
the worn paint
with
new, who
bathes the skiff
in the suds
of hope
and perfection.
Her standards
are so high
the sun has
blessed her
forehead. I
mean, she's

scorched. But
the flagstone
is freshly
sealed.
The little
engines all hum
in the steam
room—the
dishwasher
with its tiny
clacking heart,
and all
the bellies of
the laundry
stuffed with clothes.

And I wake in this house, this traveling vessel,
clean and ready for the days of my life.

∾

The God of Noah is an artist; her disappointment is an artist's
disappointment in what can be created but not controlled. How
disappointing, these awkward mirrors. How disappointing, these
river stones. These willful swaying beings, whim-wracked and
whim-wasted, all days and dazed. And how many times can you
learn to work the odd ratio of flood and hope, to declare a truce
with Imperfection.

The commandment was precise: each cubit accounted for. Her
best shot at saving what was worth saving:

a mirror
a stone
a mirror.
No. a stone.

An olive branch. A landing place. A rainbow.

∾

My Zeda, with a plumb line sense for a growing child's attention,
bought my son a multi-sided gemstone, a prism, that we could dangle
from his window on a string.

The rainbows crept out each morning at 10 o'clock, striping the floors
rainbow, rainbow painted to the walls, and every surface dotted
crystalline with the shadow of a gem dangling against the colors
like a cat's eye.

So I wore the rainbows on my arms, and my boy danced in the rainbows
with his four-year-old feet. And with this one gift that wise man found a
way to bathe us in his love and promises all the days of our lives. Even now that
he's gone unwilling from this place of storms and sunbeam, this man who
was a willing lightning rod to my struggles, whose wisdom was better than I
knew (especially when he told me my depths might just be humdrum), he
brought us together for dancing, and he taught us how to bless:

> He says: that the interplay on glass and air
> is an act of Intention
>
> A covenant we make with light and wavelength
> by what we draw near
>
> Is both science *and* sacred. We call
> not to god but Ourselves in our promises here.

❧

And so I stand with you in the holy instant . . . as near as you would have me.

❧

Is it mistaken to believe the difficult life is not a good life? Does difficulty
strip the texture from a single day?

Helen says that *Perfection is the consolation prize*
for those who can't enjoy what's going on right now.

Then three words on one branch:
Cat—Darkness—Bathtub

Shall I throw my head back into the journey?
Shall I throw my head back . . . and *laugh*?

❧

After the 40th day and the 40th night,
my breath caught in the sinew of my body.

Everything heaving together. The waters
recede, and then the dark. With a

clack and a scuffle, a broken branch
drags across the window. A winded dove

finds the avocado tree in our yard, and finds
it good, fritters with a frightened voicebox

from lawn to table. To wire. To tree again.
A skunk scampers down our driveway

with five babies keeping pace under her tail.

And here I am, finally and at last, in my
40th year, in the middle of my life

awake in my body

For I have washed your jeans and new embroidered shirt . . .

*I don't want you to do the dishes. I want you to **want** to do the dishes . . .*
from the film *The Break-Up*

For I am a lout who never does the laundry
For to please you, I have done the laundry
For I have washed your jeans and new embroidered shirt
For my sweater with them has infected your new clothes with dark blue measles
For they were sexy clothes—and make you look tough and gentle, firm enough to
    unhand a man of his guns
For your new lucky jeans turned out not to be so lucky
For I was careless. Lord was I careless.
For I rushed through the laundry.
For I neglected to separate the whites from the darks nor did I read the labels.
For sometimes I'm just like that
For I have neglected, have been negligent, Lord knows I do not finish what I have
    started
For I have once again left you home dabbing at the spots I myself created
For love itself bleeds blue
For you, my lover have the heart of a lamb
For when my blue sweater lay down with your new pants, and the new embroidered
    shirt besides, there was a quick draw and much carnage
For this comes down, in fact, to a poem about laundry
For there are always (you have said) at least eight loads and that's not counting the
    towels which are two loads and the sheets that are another
For I am the woman who has tried to do the laundry
But I would not obey
           Tumble Dry low
Nor   Wash separately
For lo, it is not enough to do the laundry. One has to want to
Handle each label like a blessing, and press each precious cuff
As if it were somebody's heart

i almost spoke i never spoke

Ode to New Leisure: Technology

Stranger let me sing your brain to sleep,
Reader, let me take you in my lap
under the army blanket from WWII
the dimestore gave you, while young faces
shimmer out of the LCD, predictable as Biblical return.

Predictable as a finger's touch return
in the evening when your day is spent.
On the percussive keyboard of an open heart,
you search for answers and the answers come
across the ethernet of everything

pointing toward a future of hope and answering
for every unspoke wish you ever washed,
numb as a cow, following the cowbells home
toward the random poetry of shopping carts.
Do not, repeat, do not sit still and *hurt*.

Predictable as a finger's touch return
someone will help you delay astonishment
in that quiet room where you, stalled, wait:
so search for answers. Let the answers come
with the random poetry of shopping carts.

So Stranger, hold that laptop in your lap
And Reader, let me sing you back to sleep
while young faces shimmer out of the LCD,
a dimestore blanket over each lost lure.
I know you're looking for an answer: that's pure

but there are some things a new car *can* cure.

Scenes Abroad

I.

At twenty in this city, I was afraid
of everything. Out of the jet's huge belly, we detached
from our own time into this other. Set down
into a foreignness I'd trembled, a new bride.
Now, in a marriage to myself that will last 60 years,
I have outlived the first chapter. My hands,
no longer so precious nor so impotent. My faults,
familiar and forgivable. My neck, laced with no
metaphors. My ears hear pretty well. Not better.

And now we can start seeing other people—
me and I. The rapture of a dome. The voice
of the contralto outside transport me but say
nothing about me. And these ancient and end-
lessly rewritten buildings: are in some ways
like me, but are neither me nor mine.

2.

A young man refinishes a 16th century door
with a knife and a ruler on the rue Belleyme.
An old man in a work coat lacquers the mortar
of a brasserie that has perked a century on his corner.

Geometries of responsibility, restoration. reinvention.
A young woman in a blue coat carries tulips
under one arm. Red to light up her 18th century flat.
The city's rituals seem bound to this rhythm:

to reinvent what you mustn't wish back.
The young lovers pepper benches in the square.
I doubt their loves will last better than mine.
But they blend together love with resilience here
We have seen dukes and stars and turpentine . . .

Serpent's Tooth

Penitent but never really clean
I hold my achy-tired sleeping child
Before 7 this morning I was screaming
over a bowl of toppled Lucky Charms

he knocked by accident from the couch's arm.
The day declined from there: "Why
are you always working so much, Mom?"
"Do we really have to go in car again?"

And I in a fog of *shush, hurry up,* and *no*
shut in a thorny internal monologue.
"Why is Daddy better at finding things?"
"Stop! Don't put those fingers on my screen!"

"But I was only going to press Return."
I hold his broken body in my arms
4 p.m. nap—sign of a spirit doused
like the fire in the grate that scared him last night

until we poured a measuring cup of water on it.
When he wakes, I'd like to think I'll get down on my knees
to listen to a long story about how the bulldozer
wants to chop a forest of peg trees.

I don't know where that other mother went?
Or how he and I can get her back?
I cringe at sticky fingers on my neck—
penitent and sorry but still wild.

On Not Aiming for What You Really Want

At Salt Creek Beach, with Elizabeth

Roots in the cliff-face.
Orange rind in my mouth.
That muted sweetness.
A difficult promise.

That rind is not the thing
itself, but its cover.
So is the cliff-face. So is this
turning backward to look at it.

So is my choice *not*
to face out over
the big riprangle of sunset
where the sun's

on a half-shell of trouble
where in the surf, surfers
bob like seals
above the mussels and coral.

They say, *not* to look
into the sun itself
but to the side of it
which is why I'm looking and looking

always past your ear. Oh, Elizabeth,
yesterday, on the radio,
an economist explained
behavioral market theory. She said,

the person
who buys
the second-to-the-least expensive
soap, always buys

the second-to-the-least
expensive car. So maybe that's
why I can't really look

right at you,
why I can't hold
every burning instant of your brightness
with my eyes.

Sapphics on Nursing

for ABB

Distance laid its static on us as mothers
Once we'd passed our rocky first spring together
Phoning news ("Bad Night!" "Poop volcano," "Lev woke
five times"), the evenings

We spent lonely pacing the kitchen, hours
We had only howling warm tender bundled
Weights, the phone, each other, and days we strolled through
Descanso Gardens.

On those paths of fallen, bruised camellias,
Rolling shade and stone under wheels of strollers,
Sleep-deprived, sore-nippled, confused and angry,
Quipping, crying, we

Shifted fussy small boys from tit to shoulder.
Sometimes I would pick up your tiny Mitchell,
Gangly small anemone—eager grin, his
Blue eyes darting. Lev

Reared determination, back arched, neck stretched
Toward his usurped position. On stone steps, we'd
Change them, trading stories of my best friend whose
First baby died in

Labor, or your sister who arced milk at her
Husband. Bought sprout sandwiches, cookies from con-
Cession, we'd plan on sharing but always went
Back for seconds. I,

Nursing, watched your son at your dewy nipple
And your blond hair beaded in orange sunbeams,
Watched your calves gain shape as months passed from labor—
I saw this wordless—

And I knew I loved your grown body fiercely
Not unlike my love for those growing babies
And the guilty intimacy of tell-all
Phone calls at midday.

As our babies started to stand and toddle,
Your hurt marriage healed with your growing Mitchell.
Month by month our phone-calling dwindled out. My
Problems continued.

Ah, Janine, time's passed. There have been such changes.
Lev starts preschool twice a week this September.
Sometimes I see boys who I think are Mitch—I'll
Have no more babies.

Sometimes I remember Descanso Gardens—
Missing noontimes spent at white plastic tables,
Telling truths we couldn't share other places
To the shrill fugue of

Bird-call, boy-call, soft urgent speech and nursing.
Underneath the clouds that would pass, the airplanes
In the darting sun of that worn-down April
Our breasts grew firm, the

Pressure drove our speaking. How I wish I'd known
That baby-season, how without consent, words, or warning
Milk entered, life claimed all those empty spaces
In us, between us.

Diptych

for Kelly

My son, singled, struck and stung,
by that unprosecutable blow, the schoolyard
skim, is such a small and serious person,
darkly deliberating interactions, skirmishes,
schoolchildren. He empties out his haul
of stories over a buttery grilled cheese dinner
on our linoleum kitchen-floor. I ask myself
if he's thinner than before. Fallen from grace,
he's still my grace, the sinewy 5-year-old
I try to rescue with love as a daily mitigation
of my separate needs, mistakes, whims.
I kiss his day-weary wholesome face.
He wipes the kiss away. Unhelped, uncertain.

The sinewy 5-year-old I tried to rescue
from my separations: need, mistake, whim
loves the creature in me I wish I weren't
when he courts the darts of school children.
Home, I try to hold myself
to his game of knights and dragons
where he likes to rewrite the rules.
But my wings are chafing against my body
and I can feel the fire breath
singeing him, as he tells the stories he drags home
from school. There is no rescue from this forest
of childhood game play and maternal
misstep and mistake. I cup the head I cherish. He smiles
at my . . . *distraction!* . . . then uncertain, he wipes the kiss away.

The Song of the Sippy Cup

In the never truly ever
truly dark dark night, ever
pink-zipped, slat-cut,
dark-parked light,
you late touch my toes
with your broad flat
own horny-nailed cold
toes. Clock-tock, wake-shock.

In the ever truly never
truly long long night, our
little snoring-snarling
wild-child mild-child
starling-darling wakes
every two, three (you-sleep)
hours, in the never truly ever
truly lawn brawn fawn dawn.

Contingency, Irony, Ingenue-ity

after Richard Rorty

The when there was: I knew Integrity.
A feathered preybird plucking marrow clean.
The splintered husk, the blue-green ocean sheen.
A thorn-toed cactus, live and boundaried.

The when I cannot say. The Why married
a sorry little girl who liked a match.
Scratch scratch pull sigh. The claw. The fiery catch.
Cindered to a twig. The parity

of shadow laid to shadow. Now a Day
has lent her blurring fingers to the rim
of every line. Of sky. The meaning dim
imperfects any whimper. Watch. I deign

to blur myself. Behooved, untruthed. The rain
makes pockets. Plants its small mouths in the dirt
like kisses. There's no there. Apart, inert
the world that is. Where opened, seed may stay.

But metaphors and idioms and birds
of prey whose claws would syllable Real out
must find the furred world can't be caught or touted.
That shadow laid to shadow is a myth.

Such freedom runs my image to the wall.
What light behind it? Backward-pointing, dotes
on absolutes. Why search for Truth at all?
How did I really mean the things I wrote?

my own sound a water

Mama

*And Jacob wakened from his
sleep ... "Indeed, this Place is a
sacred place, and I ... I did not know ..."*

I remember calling for her in the night, the sound
that began as a sound for something, for
summoning, became
(eyelids, limbs still thick with sleep) became
lazy, only a syllable
mama mama ma
In the air around my ears that gray light
like television snow
in the room around my small body
my own sound a water I could swim through
mama mama mama mama ma ma ma
just one wet note
ringed by a little spittle, the plucking effort
played on by the tongue,
the ladle of my hope spooning that one wish
over and over
spinning
up and down
inside the me-circle
mouth-lips
a kind of ball
a light
a swinging,
until I wasn't calling *for*,
I was just calling *out*
filling the dark with myself
wholly, achingly
all pure intention with
the innocence still on it
not a single unwishing in my way:
I was just I speaking
the truest I I ever spoke.

Pep Talk

for LBD, and her threads

My dearest Jenny Factor
only you are going to decide what next you are going to do
so for a moment don't think about your motherfathersisterbrother
and give it a rest about global warming hardwork late-nights the ambition-and-
    frustration of concentration
instead think about Peter Lai's
fabrics
the lungs in his skirts, the breath in his crinolines,
that thin lavender skin, that blue flame cloth,
Think, if you must,
how one fabric is like canvas whipped into meringue, pink flowers beaded to the
    rucksack
about how, on his heavy yellow silks, there are ridges and marks like bark
Then think of that small man late at night
on a squat stool
in the L shaped throat of his shop
racks of trim and buttons behind him higher than his head
think how late it is
so late
the night opens its hours like a button-shirt
the lamp spilling extravagantly
over the bosom of the fabrics,
while Peter leans in closer
like he's listening
and, Jenny, don't you see
how un-alone he is
dear one
like he's teasing out some joy
the materials animate under those nimble old fingers
making, as he touches them, a swoosh, or a crinkle,
a yawn, a gasp, each with their own sigh, their own kind of simper
and he, that small man, a smile just above his needle
lets all their possibilities go chordal

every night
just like this one
stitching
one unexpected syllable
to the next

A Mother's Headache

The room, a choke of twilight
—he enters with a tray—
toward that hill-high blob, all-covered,
he whispers, "*Can I stay?*"
The air, hot as fear
The walls, slicked with silk
Who knows what he may hear
from that tortured chink of quilt?

Though he fly to the far-off Negev
where sands sting at his cheeks like salt,
though he kneel on a powerless skiff in the dark
praying the sea storms stop,
though he drain a glass of fruity mash
from a bar table near Chernobyl
he will never once stand so far off from home
as that bed that has swallowed his mother

Descent to the Pt. Reyes Lighthouse

Wedded less
to a husband than to this
long habit of a checked wistfulness,

she descends
the three hundred steps
leaning her body into the wind.

Wind on the promontory,
wind, wind, the shore made sorry
and the land, and the sea, twisted with worry

so that no jacket,
no scarf, no tourist racket,
can keep wind out of the place fear's packed in.

Moaning timber.
The sea cliffs shudder,
the eerie hummed lines of telephone wires.

Iceplant and poppy
on the hill are dripping
with spray, yet, seem brightly happy

like those other
people hurrying down, the lovers,
the mother keeping her small boys from pushing each other,

the level Midwesterners,
even-tempered as cows, the Easter
vacation crowd from some school with a Pastor.

At the bottom stair
is the wide point where
red flags and sea breakers say "Beware."

On the spit,
the lighthouse sits,
battered by Pacific salts.

The high tower
lifts, presiding over
that margin where the sea wields its power.

Inside, a wall
mural tells the long tale
of the man who tended the lighthouse through squalls

and storm,
sending the pale warning
into months of chilly winter mornings

lacking food,
lacking comfort, short on wood,
with no company except the chaos, he brooded

and wrote
his diary notes.
Got madder and stranger, got

remembered
by the lovers, their finger-
knotted hands holding everything together,

reading,
his wall, standing,
laughing at the quotes she could be writing

herself. Better,
the girl in a green sweater
hair short as a boy's, who smiles past her.

So she climbs
the lighthouse tower, finds
the windy skirt where sound gives way to silence, time,

the wind,
the sea breakers. Pinned
to the frame of the tower, she owns her sins,

she thinks,
How weak, how tireless
is that circling light, enduring its loneliness.

Then a bell
sends its wail
out of the windy place it's settled

till from the sea,
a ship's horn sounds brightly
to She Who Stays from She Who Totters Free.

Beyond the lip
of railing, the cliffs
shimmer, the sun glints

off all she sees.
Every choice bobs up like buoys,
dips and churns, rebounds, runs free

out into the
tumbling, icy
grasping reach of sea, sea, sea.

Death Valley Pupfish

Nevertheless,
the blind pupfish burst open
into the sometime stream,
dodging pebbles,
wiggling away from shadows,
darting back and forth
through the dusty water.
She wonders
how many eggs
lie waiting in places
the water never touches.
She wonders
how they decide
or do they
to throw their live bodies out
into the flowing streamers,
the warm scarves
of water
that exist haphazardly,
and run,
for awhile,
across the desert pavement,
that exist uncertainly,
like her poems,
or her marriage,
like any stream
She'd hoped
would teem
with life

Notes from the Other Side

oh pray that what we want
is worth this running
pray that what we're running
toward
is what we want.

from lucille clifton,
"we are running"

Knotted as the
hands of prayer, we
rode the uptown

down where we
stood near, near waiting the rough
and tumble let-down

in the Bowery. I've heard,
any woman happy
in the a.m. was

suicidal the day
before, depression
making the only

opening. But I was
already breathing
out air I carved

for myself
mole   tunnel   light, when
you came

and we laughed into
mauve halter tops,
breasts

popping up through
spandex with all
the helpless

energy of crocuses.
Blades along the river,
steady contact

of wheels. City Spring.
Estival. In that
strange restaurant, La Nouvelle

Justine,
a blonde pinned
herself

to the wall, banded
blind with silky
un-being, as friends

fingered and rolled
her bared hillsides,
nipples plucked up,

as new eyes,
her nude backside, feathered,
paddled

in waves.
We wandered home
past that damp

chasm
its drugged liquid silver
in our veins.

Rod-taught with
expectancy, near—
not-near, on the edge

of doing,
doing . . .
Sex is not a particularly

good reason
to live a life,
or leave one, or change one.

You and I, love,
are old friends
who sometimes

bring each other
to the verge
but never over. Moses

looking down
into some Promised Land,
a hopeful/hopeless

expectancy, as
unlooked for
as is Joy. Sun-

swallowed and rising,
in the next
dawn, Kissed Fingers,

you were gone. But
I own Manhattan. I am
roughly the size of a

skyscraper.
Liberty kneels
at my feet.

Settling In

How she loved
each bare floor, each
naked wall, the shadows on

newly empty halls.
By day, her head humming
to itself of dreams, she cleaned and

scrubbed
to make life
new; dislodging from the corner,

the old
moths and cicadas
pinned to the screen, the carcasses

of grasshoppers
dangling from beams,
and each window sill's clutter of

dried beetles
and dead bees. But,
through each opening, each closing door,

the old life
returns on six legs, or
spins a musty web as it roosts over

a poison pot, or
descends from above
to drink blood in. This is how it

happens: the
settling in—the press
of wilderness returns to carved-out space, to skin.

twice i grew that tiny heart

Amma's Love Lesson

the hug, for Cristin

In a hotel room where the carpet
is red, is garish, where light fluoresces
humanlit and windowless

A woman keeps opening
her arms
keeps opening
her arms keeps opening her
chest
her mouth her heart
like butter
spread
on bread
like a button
slipped from its eye—she
keeps opening and opening

the little warmth
of Now
Feel how
the opulence of her
opens and opens
There is the sense of paper
of cardamom
The scent of pepper
the coal, the sweet sweat,

And she keeps opening
her warmth and opening her warmth
until the room is
a place that summer
comes into
and singing comes out of

like a huge box
like a goose's wing
the warm underside
of everything. In this hotel room

a woman keeps opening.

Ode to Old Leisure: Of Boredom

It starts in an emptiness that telescopes
      toward a hot whiteness in the humid air.

It must find focus—triceratops
      or a lady's glowing milk-brown hair.

The body loves absence
            the body wise—
luxuriates in a goldfish O
      There is no innocence, only . . . slowing . . .

the perfect tintinnabulation of air, and oh
      over here
          and old very very
a space of nothing, those smoking stacks of books,

      cascading
          when they walk can sift
the introspection that clings to Lack.

Oh thinker, professor
      hear me here: I want the empty eras back
I want the 17th Century dusk, the streets that smell
      of soot and sack

      and carriage wheels that turn on track:
Contemporary Time, a Labrador, rolls on His back
      for us to scratch. Run, practitioner, run the field

till all the wheat will light and catch.

The Phone Call

From the depressed sunshine of this dusty spring,
suddenly halos of jacaranda.
Lavender puddles, lavender clouds.
So startling, I wonder where my head has been.
(Sneaked up upon.)

I noticed "our" trees while I was outside driving
through the car's antiseptic window, and
it looks as if sanctity poured down purple tenderness
for some rough crowds to trample on.
(But no, the blossoms are still whole trumpets.)

So I imagine the clumsy wood castanets, labial lips parting,
an unassuming tree trunk tandem, and
how one little girl called the pods
turtle shells, and a woman I know wrote poems about them, and how in
the sandbox (was it three springs ago?),

our son, newly bipedal, spent a morning
looping, carrying tiny purple blooms in a plastic bucket, and
a second small girl who did not speak many words
helped him, her sleek black hair drawn
behind her ears (like reined excess).

You were there, reading, thinking.
Surely in two weeks, these purple heavens will be browned, a
crease through the heart of each blossom. So how
come when you said you were seeing someone
(after your long, respectable delay),

I heard the purple bruising, blooming
in your voice, and all through that phoned up
conversation, I remembered those other words
we said many springs ago down
on a pavement (forgotten?).

165 Cambridge Park Drive, Day 2

for my son, after a poem by Alicia Ostriker

I pause for a moment to laugh at myself:
Not three hours after I told you:

"When you're out running, Honey, be careful of ticks,"
I find myself wanting to text you back the opposite:

Sweetheart, there is a field near the new apartment
Come join me! It's filled with bunnies. I'm standing in

*grasses tickling my shin*s. Brown field rabbits
in lazy hop, just a yawn at the base of the shafts. And above,

tiny brown birds chirp and pop, and one red-wing is
winging from tip to tip, her touch lighting the twilight like a flame.

Darling, I have been terrified for days.
I couldn't help but warn you about something.

I have been alone, driving fast on streets
unfamiliar.

I have been unloading boxes as heavy as
myself into and out of cars.

I have been shopping and buying my way
toward knowledge, toward controlling something.

I have been second-guessing myself: the new cost
of eggs, the apartment I chose so quickly for

this cross country move. And then, I catch
myself here, at the edge of a rainy field:

And I want to make you promise to take
your bike here into the wildness

I want to make you promise, sun on your bare
legs, to run and run. *Oh mother,* I imagine you

mock: *"Be safe." "Be surefooted." How
am I supposed to do both at the same*

time? Oh dear, please forgive me, won't you?
Didn't you once say to your father

that Consistency is overrated?
So I am a mother like every other:

one hand pushes you forward, while the
other is all stop sign. But look. Here's what

I'm really saying. I am terrified
80 times each hour, but moving out into the grasses

anyway because I want to know what's here.
My advice isn't wisdom. Just footnotes

to a text I'm still writing, dispatches from
life's field office, postcards from a battlefield

of desire and fear. Listen, darling: the headline isn't
I'M TERRIFIED. The headline is: I'M HERE.

there is no end to it

Recitativo

After a friendship's year of stitching
stories patiently, in itchy
wool coats, in coffeehouses,
on subway stairs, on nubbed couches
I look up from changing a CD
as you walk out to your living
room from a muffle of dressing
in a stark white string strap T

and I think: bird boy stone.
Later, backlit before a microphone
you kaleidoscope, in and out
of woman, pained then pleased,
in and out of dulcet-voiced brain
holding her own at faculty teas.
Some nights, I wonder about
the two sides of your nude beauty,

imagine a gash's continent
bold fingers would see, a cleaned
ground, a survivor's testimony,
set beside your one plaint-
ive syllable, the egg-yolk of a girl's tit.
Walking, your coat flies open. I take it
like a whip. Whispers of what a body
whispers. I don't (won't) answer it.

She Said to Me

The difference between the lived life and the slept life
is not the chipped ivory picture frame hung—or not hung—on the wall,

or choosing to bring home the periwinkle bra
instead of the white one—

The difference is a quality of attention. The difference is
always knowing where Death is. Misplace death,

and the ants in your kitchen matter, you'll care
that there are crumbs in your child's bed, her hair

needs a trim, and your socks don't match.
The slept life dithers on in a kind of otherly-

centered attention like a Viking compass, a lode stone afloat
in a bowl on a boat, bobbing directional yet directionless,

personally landless, othering othering—
The slept life repels like North to North, retells like

your lover's favorite story, unspells like a malaprop
you chose only because it rhymes.

Well, if that's the difference
between the slept life and the lived life, I asked her,

Have we misplaced Death, or *Laughter*?

Letter in (. . .), Threes, Fives, and Sixes

Last night, I dreamed my mind
slipped its configuration
and dived inside your dream.
A searing interrelation
of spirits under the seam.
(I slipped into your dream!)

It's bound to end with trouble.
Someone feeling rejected.
Good china in the rubble
much as the crowds expected
the day I blew soap bubbles

with my little guy in the park.
I wished my feelings were Other
in the gloom of a Saturday dark
descending on children & lovers.
The apple tree rose, a stark

reminder of HerStory's sin:
the spontaneous urge to Give In.
Let feminists blast me but note
how like the prostitute,
I'd take the dick in my throat

(though don't put that in a quote),
I'd even give up the Vote
for the pleasure of forcing a stretch
and wanting what isn't quite right
rather than wait out an Itch.

Obsession isn't love
though it can add some Flavor.
And nurture isn't erotic
though tell that to my liver
the briny morning after
when a friend arrives with the seltzer.

A woman my age should be smarter
knowing a sign's marked Danger.
When a friend reminds me of Mother,
I probably shouldn't write her
four times a day for starters . . .

I cannot force a knot.
I can't evade the lack.
I can't remove the spot
from my beige linen slacks,
or the kiss of the parking lot
from my lunch-seated ass.

But I'd yank a life to mine
with another ether letter.
Though words return like breath
and calm like a glass of water,
in the end, it's only ether.

And there's nothing new where I live
nor anything under the sun
in this stale August heat
that I am wishing on.
Just the dead still life of my street
with summer wearing on.

There's a rue where a street's ripped up
and trucks lay down new road,
and a life begins again
in the sound of steam and spade.
My letters find someone home
in friendship, less alone.

I think this is all for the good.
I think this is all for the good.

Pen Pals

for Julie, who believed in this poem

Right now I like you best when you are flat
on paper, scrolled in ether messages,
and on white sheets, ink-stained, addressed and stamped.

In humid rooms, so awkward I get cramps,
we sip in silence, swap book passages.
Far better, white sheets, ink-stained, addressed, stamped

to tear open in leisure and get damp,
on sometime-thoughts of sweet permissages
or real world talk more intimate than flat.

Granted, you're not ambiguous. You prattle
like a girl, "Then she . . ." these discourses
come on white quartered sheets, ink-stained and stamped.

No mad provacatrix. But damn! You pack
a punch in phrases, scrapbook images
until I'm sure I'd like you to be flat-

tered by the way such scribbles make romance.
Let words do what hands do: console, caress,
on folded sheets. Our dailiness gets stamped

to bear no risk of touch. I won't play tramp
to loose your stiff boy though I'm capable
—would probably even like it quite well—flat,
on white sheets, undressed, ink-stained, licked like stamps.

Romantic Friendship

She's gone home. The bundle of logs she brought
are now ashes in the fireplace. Three bare
spots where cinders bit the carpet, hissing and tunneling
into the liner like sand beetles after a tide.
It will take half an hour to re-file the pile
of books pulled from my shelves to mark
things we said or did or meant.
Over the dining table—
a tent; the first cloth I've laid on it in weeks
(a child could hide behind or underneath)
And two meals' dishes make ramshackle
beach huts in the sink.

               After I click shut
the door behind her, the dishes washed—
After the house and its ghosts are mine again,
I pass the vacuum's long throat
over the ashes around the hearth,
and a blonde-bellied spider shimmies out of the ash,
like a moving ash. I
almost suck her in, swallowing down
her escape; but stop to watch her waddle
up the side away. Homeward, I suppose. And
I imagined her life, her nest.

Every day now, it seems I'm discovering
this other gentler way: how letting

what matters go, some part I need most, stays.

Spider

I am a belly in the dark.
Between the glass and storm window,
I keep vigil near my sack.

heat   heat   heat. The summer longs
to lengthen out beyond my strength.

Iridescent, beating things.
I eat the quiet moths that land
I let them fall, husks,

and wings, still air moving
under glass.
The window sill grows rank. This death

One dawn with legs above the sack,
beige spillage, moving dots, a mass.
I keep my watch. They slip outside

                           through cracks
and make a lens in cracks.
Twice I grow

that tiny heart,
where I wait, translucent, skinned.
I am a belly in the dark,

eating. What I hunger from
never stops for birth
                           or death.
and so
I cling, spider-blessed.

Nest (recipe)

for Eloise Klein Healy

Beaked bags   Ho dep
me pot   Bi lo   Confetti of commerce
Pillow stuffing   Black net
from under grave-
L Grass limp from garden's
Edge ungainly gawky No
Nest niceties   What's avail
able   Is enough

Reciprocal?

Mouse, this strange intensity of light
through the high thick windows'
reading glass and your heavy grief
aches my head like a book I read all night.
And I think the sun is beginning to read us too
like eyes that suddenly realize we are here,
talking on as the sundown draws in near.

Pressures in the head and in the world are mutual,
and there is a gravity-pull between two people
whether or not it's effectual
even to try to stroke away your grief—
my head to your shoulder, your thin body's mute
deciding whether to yield, to hold stiff,
or to lean. What do I feel

through my third headache in as many days
not even beginning to understand
why I can now describe six ways
a smile passes your face?

You do not read me any more
than a book would read its reader,
though I would guess
your friends watch and interpret nonetheless,

as friends will do.
And I wouldn't mind knowing really
whether or not I love you
in one or another definition of the word;
although I would do nothing about it,
through your grief's dust-jacket
but talk until midnight
and let this book close.

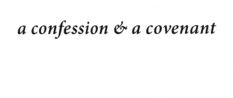

a confession & a covenant

Passing Through

for Reginald Shepherd, who closed his emails "Peace and Poetry"

This morning, a Hadron collider
recreating
the birth of a universe.
Tonight: nothing. Crickets. A distinctly human silence.
There is a hole in the universe, the astrologers say,
blaming the big machine, and I believe them.
I take out the trash. I fall through.
There, by the trashbins, beside the garage.
Night on my shoulders,
chilly air beating against my hair.

The day slows long enough to listen, and so
hours after the phone call,
the call catches up to me.
Reginald? Where are you? A distinctly human silence.

You were the night's face of doing, glistened with sweat.
You had instructions for the rain, for the moon.
The spiders have instructions too. For the rain,
For the moon. They are always so busy
at their work. So ongoing.

And I, who am always going, am now
A distinctly human silence
And you, so you, glistening with the sweat of doing
were every map I ever read about this work—
A hole in the universe. A hole in the whole unwise universe.
I am standing in it. And you. You stopped. But I can see you here.

For many years, the poet busied herself . . .
with cars and roads and McDonald's happy meals
with mothers and lovers and toddlers and teachers
with the woman on the train, the man on the subway
For many years the poet busied herself with everything
not herself
Anxiety a quiet buzz that soothed her and never left her
For many years she did not recognize the pre cognate child
always lost and thinking
inside her
While all along the other poets were gathered on the spot
They were not waiting for anything
They were simply
birds, settled on a lake
(Waiting not even for flight,
for flight. *O wings of my body, open open.*)
For years there was bread and syntax between them,
while the poet ordered up her meal local
all commerce and content,
lonely and lazy.
                    Where was the cóntent? The contént?
Where there is flight, where there is
no waiting for flight, no anxiety about flight . . .
where is that?

～

Now I am coming late to the edge of this lake
Won't you find me a little room, Reginald
fold up some wing, slide over
So that we can sit
where the shore is wet in the aftermath of tide
dragged rocks and a disaggregate of sand
this bouquet of thingyiness and un-imagining,
from which you turned Peace into Poetry
Here at last let's slice the bread like time
Let's hem and hedge in the
space between us
There is—there has always been—so much blue

This is the lake and the poets are gathered.
Each face, a moon of a face, hanging open
toward—what?—how cold
the lake is and the very depth
of blue, a candlewax and the sweet smell
of smoke after the light goes out
And the lake, on its enormous web of roots . . .

But you are not here, as much as I wish you were
Alone, I hear the breath inside me and then
all is heartbeat heart heart beat   heart beat
How have I at last arrived
in poetry, genderless as once you saw me,
one rush and uneasy laugh away
Dark now the swirling motions on the lake, in my hair
a clinking in the branches, damp leaves against skin,
and at last, I have given myself this time for wading and for waiting in!
from the shore, on this little nest of rock,

I imagine you by my side
Nests of shame, of failure, of disappointment,
Of scrap and skin,
nests of how friendship might have softened us
Reginald, where are you?
I have found the spot
I am still here sitting on
this nest of Might Have Been.

People Ask What I Do

for Elena, with love

And I wish I were doing anything else:
Chopping giant blocks of ice near the north pole in the arctic
Or driving a truck on a two-lane highway
over the grapevine in California
Battling bulls
Or pulling my hair out, one string at a time.

Ahh Poetry, they say and smile
as if they were talking about their adorable
four-year-old in a princess costume.

I wonder if they know the same *Poetry*
I know: the one who beats me up in back alleyways. The one
who calls my name as if it's
some kind of slur. Poetry.

Poetry is dear and vast and glitters,
while I am neither big
nor bright nor clever. And I long ago
stopped waiting for my crown.
I just haul these poems the way
a coal miner hauls coal:

one raw, unprocessed load at a time.

Joanna at 2 o'clock

after painter Euan Uglow (1932–2000), BBC interview on
"Root Five Nude" whose model was named Joanna
(Uglow quotes italicized)

Joanna at 8 a.m., 9, 10, even noon—
      the buses pass by, the taxis, the light—she is all raked over.

She becomes red for a moment, or blue. But that's no good: it's the pink
      I'm after. Do you see it?   There!   On the little nub

of her heel, the *hyperextended* knee, and then differently
      Here! at midcalf where the razor stopped

—all the suss and intonations of that *rose*.

Who can get magic moments in six hours a day? I'll ask you
      that question. I ask you that! *You get a few*

magic moments in a week! The same thing
      happens with the light, but Joanna at 2 o'clock—

sometimes *she becomes magical.* It's *when you get to see the idea*
      almost happening in front of you.

Her left knee just so—
      half-gaged up to capture my mark on the blue board. Her right foot

tossed away, as far out as I can ask her to go. See
      how she must work

      with her whole leg until with a wiggle it hops into position
and There!   Above: the mons

falls open. The pubis—that mauve patch—
　　Then she wraps her fingers around the one nail I hammered hard

into the board. Head flipped onto an elbow; wakeful. See the lines
of it. *At times*

one has to make a thing go much further and then paint it out. That's how
　　I remember watching her

　　　　in my dream, on the chair in the lobby,
　　　　her breath so close he could eat it. And he,
　　　　stopping suddenly: the wet　"you want this—"
　　　　And she: "your finger, all the way in there　now"
　　　　and they'd ride together the cruise, the cream

But what she was after was before. It was his full weight, the heavy sack of him
　　upon her, the lobby open, those catwalk eyes

and me watching as she discovered again and again
　　the rich wreckless rinsing-through

of the body's own making.
　　　　　　We think　the let down can save us.

But it is rather　every messy incursion rising
　　from outside the self's own foam.

Everything in the painting can be violated. Everything is in position
　　to be destroyed.

At times, one has to make a thing to find the very outer limit
　　like walking the perimeter of a field in the dark.

You can fix three things that are wrong, but try to fix
        all five and the painting fails.

She *makes the emergency.*   She, Joanna. I make the measurements on
        an indigo board.   Then wine shattering against the floor.

I find that I don't drop an idea easily. The painter and the model
        are in crisis.

I need her desperately, she knows that as well as I do. And *she* needs . . .
        . . . I don't know what she needs . . .

But our crisis is somehow parallel and alike.

Malibu Noël

for JA and MF

Christmas house of roasting rosemary, incense,
and the siren ocean whose song is sunset,
shaping wing and wave in the moment's treason:
daylight is falling.

Falling day, the sun with no sense of season
topples westward, splattering rose and ripple.
Eastward, lights respond to new night like dimmer
switches dragged upward.

In the low tide's clear-washed wet sand of evening,
doors swing wide, and families with their children
in red sweaters, lace, patent-leathers squeaking,
take to the beach. Their

German shepherds, Huskies flash teeth and wrangle,
nosing sand, they race through the posts of neighbors.
Carpeting their fur in their play, they chase raw
seaweed like strangers.

From the tide-toed edges, a small boy bundles
with his shovel, waddling toward the wood stairs,
and his mother follows him with her scarf tied
against the wind chill.

There are those who make of such nights a goblet.
There are those who celebrate how the glimmer
of a live room closes up warm and sacred,
lives filled with children.

All my life, my strange eyes have seen the wrong things.
Missing one thing, settling on another.
Wiping up graffiti from sides of boulders,
clearing, erasing

Bald sunrise eclipsing the ashen woman
wandering on the sand with a mothy blanket.
Mimicking a mood, my perspective shifts off,
listless, mistaken.

"This is how I see," said Picasso pointing
to a canvas, Cubism's altered women,
"Sight's sequential, subject to subject feeling."
Eyes plucked like nipples.

So here's looking west where the day's upended
like a toddler's punch, and the curlews argue
over fish. I keep to my back the shadows
milling around us.

Mirror of the pool shows a neighbor's perfect
pine extending ten feet and globed like bread fruit.
In the kitchen, seventy years is kneading
fresh loaves for dinner.

One can almost hear every wineglass set down
on the table, vibrating from its landing.
At the moment hands let an object settle,
everything's shaken.

Doors unlock, the families call their wandering
parties home and close up the house for nightfall.
Every staircase takes on its load of footsteps.
Let's watch the riptide.

Houses perch like nests on the seacliff. Houses,
camp fires on the bank of this primal endzone.
Shut inside, the season plays out its final
trumpet of yule time.

Christ but how the sky is a finished perfect
thought. Rose marred to amethyst in the knife fall.
All I may not choose to see in the margins
calls me to dinner.

Against Publishing

after Fleur Adcock

I write in praise of the solitary act
of *not* polishing, pressuring, or probing . . .
No rude words forcing meek words into high noon
No hope racing out the door, hastily re-robing.
Being: just that. And also, to avoid all eyes
and all the I's the wrong mind bandies out:

those imaginary looking-down-ons like an owl's,
or the bat's faint echolocation of *because* and *about*.
Rather, ear to the ground, let the loose page lie
limpid and draughty. Horseman, *pass by*.

Isn't it about time you inhabit that space of making
past meeting, past the hope of meeting, past agony or age.
Listening to the faucet, feeling the back aching
like a painter who dwells two hours on a square of beige.
No meaning but in things. No journey. No hurrying back.
Here or nowhere, shouldn't we *make peace with the fact*.

There is much to be said for Emily's fascicles,
stuffing those lonely papers in a rickety drawer,
Gertrude's epistles to Alice, the Hemingway suitcase
lost to the oblivion of the subway floor.

Morris Eaves says it well, about "the absent present".
To know the poem's hopeless in the end
the wished for communion is certainly much warmer
over coffee, in therapy, or sleeping with a friend.
I advise you then to let down all encumbrance.
Live boldly, write often, but let the poem go.

Oh lace of the snowflakes that vanish on the journey,
and leave in the mind: a murmuring of snow.

Notes

Page 23: The title, "Sinking," used as a pun for the every day tragedy of quotidian love and dishes comes from a poem by J.P. Dancing Bear, originally published in *Inner Cities of Gulls* (Salmon Poetry, 2010). Bear's work often entwines other writers in these intimate poem conversations.

Page 24: Epigraph from Rainer Maria Rilke's "Sonnets to Orpheus II, 29" as translated (and wisely adapted) by Joanna Macy, and as curated as part of Krista Tippett's episode of *On Being*, called "A Wild Love for the World."

Page 31: "The rock that turns back water like regret" echoes a line from Robert Frost's "West-Running Brook," the book which convinced me I would one day want to be a poet.

Page 40: Kay Ryan has a poem, "Carrying a Ladder," which uses the titular item symbolically. Her ladder inspired mine.

Page 97: The double "I" in the Bible verse also appears in the Hebrew original. It has been interpreted many ways. To me, it is both a stutter of not being grown into oneself yet, and a calling oneself forward, an authenticity.

Page 115: Alicia Ostriker's poems to adult daughters ring though mine to a young adult son.

Page 127: Modern city nests sometimes contain the wisps and weavings of what we would think of as trash: shopping bags, twist-ties, and other articles.

Page 132: "O wings of my body, open open" echoes a line from Randall Jarrell in "Woman in the Washington Zoo," in which the woman wants to open are bars of her body, not the wings.

Page 136: Euan Uglow's work method was famously slow and rigorous, sometimes extending well over a decade on a single work. This made keeping a model, for whom each painting set and concept was customized, especially difficult. This poem is about his work with a model named Joanna, an ultimately failed aesthetic partnership explored on film. BBC interview quotes from documentary "Root Five Nude" in *unbolded italics*.

Pages 139-141: The "Christmas" and "rosemary" in the first line of "Malibu Noël" repeat in a disassembled cubism near the close of the poem.

Page 142: "Against Publishing" takes its title from Fleur Adcock's ironic "Against Coupling" (which begins, "I write in praise of the solitary act."). Also echoing in the poem is W.B. Yeats' "Under Ben Bulben," Mary Oliver's "No Voyage," and William Carlos Williams' famous quote, "No ideas but in things." Morris Eaves (in a talk at the Huntington Library) has imagined a typology of "the absent present" that spins out from Derridean or Foucauldian postmodernisms.

Biographical Note

Jenny Factor is an archaeologist of object and mind, a feminist, a mother, and a dog-lover. An inhabitant of doubled geographies, Jenny helps to organize the monthly Caltech Poetry Lunch while studying eighteenth-century women's poetry networks at Brandeis University. Her first collection, *Unraveling at the Name* (Copper Canyon Press), won the Hayden Carruth Award and was a finalist for the Lambda Literary Award. Christina Pugh writes of that volume in *Poetry*, Jenny's "verse forms sing with idiosyncrasy." Factor's poems and reviews have appeared in more than a dozen anthologies, including *Poetry 180* and *The Best American Erotic Poems* (Scribner, 2008), and in *Prairie Schooner*, the *Gay & Lesbian Review*, and the *Paris Review*. Her work has been supported by an Astraea Grant in poetry and acknowledged with a Dorothy Sargent Rosenberg honorable mention. Jenny serves as Lecturer in Poetry at Caltech and is the former core faculty member in Poetry at the MFA in Creative Writing program at Antioch University Los Angeles, a writing program devoted to literature and social justice. She divides her time between Pasadena, California, and Marblehead, Massachusetts.

9 781636 281643